CARAVAN

RECIPES

compiled by
Simon Haseltine

*A selection of easy camping
and caravanning recipes to feed
a hungry family of four, using
nothing more than a camping
stove in the middle of nowhere…*

*Illustrated with
nostalgic caravanning
photographs*

SALMON

Index

With thanks to Andrew Jenkinson – caravan/motorhome journalist and historian
for sourcing the images used in this publication.

Printed and Published by Dorrigo, Manchester, England. © Copyright.

Campfire Breakfast

If you're lucky enough to be able to build a campfire, what better way than to wake up to this cooked breakfast… and no frying pan to wash too!

Good quality tin foil
8 rashers bacon (good quality from butchers)
4 cheese slices (halved)
4 large mushrooms (sliced)
2 Large beef tomatoes (sliced)
4 thin slices black pudding (sliced)

Place alternate layers of bacon, cheese, mushrooms, tomatoes and black pudding in foil. Wrap well and place in embers of fire for 20 minutes. Check if cooked and serve with a mug of campfire tea…

Breakfast All Wrapped Up

This is a great way to enjoy your breakfast sitting on the ground outside your tent in the cool morning dew – buy some wonderful home produced chutney, sausages, bacon and black pudding from your local farmer's market and enjoyed best with a mug of tea…

Pack wraps	**4 sausages**
Jar of chutney from local farmer's market	**4 slices black pudding**
6 eggs	**4 Chestnut mushrooms**
4 rashers of bacon	**2 tomatoes (halved)**

Hard boil eggs, cool, peel and roughly chop. Chop bacon, sausages, black pudding and mushrooms into bite-size pieces and fry until cooked. Spread some of your delicious chutney from the farmer's market on to the wraps (try and find some delicious aubergine chutney), fill with egg and fried mixture. Wrap and enjoy.

No fridge – use tinned baked beans with sausages, tinned mushrooms and tinned bacon grill (sliced and fried), with some fresh tomatoes.

Vegetarian – use more mushrooms, some vegetarian sausages and add walnuts.

Campsite Warden's Eye

I'm sure the campsite warden would certainly keep an eye on this breakfast dish…

4 slices thick bread   **2 tomatoes, sliced**
4 eggs   **4 rashers bacon, chopped**
Mushrooms, chopped

With a pastry cutter, cut a circle in the middle of each slice of bread. Fry these circles both sides until brown and set aside. Fry the mushrooms, tomato and bacon until cooked, then also set aside and keep warm. Fry one side of the bread slices until they are brown, turn over and crack an egg into the hole, cover and fry until cooked. Spoon mushroom, tomato and bacon mixture onto the small rounds of fried bread and serve together with the large slice of fried bread and egg.

Lumpy Cottage Pie

*No oven on camp – no problems. Try this version of your family favourite
to keep those outdoor hunger pains at bay…*

1¼ lb. minced beef	**Gravy granules**
1 large red onion (finely chopped)	**Worcestershire sauce**
1 cup peas (fresh, frozen or tinned)	**Pinch mixed herbs**
1 beef stock cube	**2 teaspoons rolled oats**

12 small new potatoes (chopped)

Fry off the onion for a few minutes, then add the mince, stock cube and herbs
to brown. Drain off any excess fat. Add a touch of Worcestershire sauce, a
little water and gravy granules to make a thick consistency. Add peas and oats,
stir and simmer for 20 minutes, adding a little water as required. In the
meantime, cube potatoes and boil until tender. Drain potatoes and add to
mince mixture for an additional 5 minutes or so. Serve with seasonal vegetables
and some crusty bread.

No fridge – use tinned mince with onions; you can also use tinned garden peas
and potatoes and serve with tinned carrots to make an equally wholesome
supper.

Campfire Supper

*How about this delicious supper cooked in the embers of a camp fire,
with a choice of puddings too. And no washing up…!*

**4 large baking potatoes   4 eggs   A little grated cheese
2 bananas   2 oranges   Pack chocolate buttons   2 chocolate mint wafers
Pack cocktail sticks   Good quality foil**

Cut top third off each potato and save. Scoop out hole in larger section of
each potato, add a little grated cheese and then break an egg into hole. Remove
any excess 'white', replace lid and seal with cocktail sticks. Double wrap in foil
and place in embers for between 45 mins and an hour until cooked (check with
a cocktail stick). Serve with warm baked beans cooked over the camp fire.

For pudding, peel banana along one side and poke chocolate buttons into
banana flesh. Reseal banana skin, wrap with foil and bake in embers for 10
minutes. Likewise, cut orange almost in half and insert a chocolate mint wafer.
Reseal with a cocktail stick, wrap in foil and bake in embers for 10 minutes.

Hungry Hotpot

Don't consign stews and hotpots to the winter months – this makes a quick and filling supper for a wet and chilly night sitting in your tent...

2 tins stewing steak in gravy   1 large onion (chopped)
1 large baking potato (thinly sliced)
Selection of local vegetables from the Farmer's Market (chopped)
(carrots, courgettes, runner beans, swede all work well)
Handful of red lentils and pearl barley   Beef stock cube
Water and gravy granules to thicken stock
Pinch mixed herbs

Simmer the lentils and pearl barley in water. Fry the onion in a little oil, then add the prepared vegetables and herbs and stir fry for a few minutes. Add the drained lentils and pearl barley and stir. Add the stewing steak and stock and cover with sliced potato and simmer gently for 30 minutes. Serve with new potatoes and some fresh chunky bread.

Sausage Pasta

My children call this 'Dad's Pasta' and it is one of our favourite camping supper dishes –
serve outdoors with, of course, with a glass or two of red wine. Delicious…

Dried Pasta (sufficient for 4 people)   **2 tins chopped tomatoes**
1 large salami sausage (no fridge variety)   **Pinch mixed herbs**
1 large red onion   **4 cloves garlic**
5 oz. mushrooms   **Olive oil**

A little red wine

Fry the onion in the olive oil for a few minutes, add the sliced salami, mushrooms, herbs and garlic. Stir-fry for 10 minutes, then add a little red wine and tinned chopped tomatoes. Simmer for a further 10 minutes. In the meantime, boil pasta in accordance with pack instructions, then drain. Place cooked pasta in large bowl, add salami mixture over top and fold in. Serve with a green salad, tomatoes and some olive bread…

No fridge – none required, a perfect camping recipe.

Chicken Casserole

Camping in the spring and autumn is great fun and this one-pot meal
will certainly help to keep the family warm…

1 lb. cooked chicken (most supermarkets sell)
1 can condensed chicken soup   Large cup peas (frozen)
Small red pepper, chopped   Rice (2 oz. per person)
Chicken or vegetable stock cube   Water

Mix the chicken, peas, pepper, rice in to the soup, add the stock cube and cook gently for 20 minutes until the rice is tender. Add a little water as required and serve with some crusty bread.

No fridge – use tinned chicken and tinned peas.

Meat & Potato Pie

The lack of a camp oven won't hinder you making this delicious meat pie with a potato topping…

1 lb. steak, cubed	**A little ale (go on, he's not looking!)**
4 oz. mushrooms	**Beef stock cube**
1 small red onion (chopped)	**Gravy granules**
	Pinch mixed herbs

4 large potatoes   Spring onions   Tomatoes (sliced)

Fry off the onion for a few minutes, add the steak and stock cube and brown. Add the mushrooms and herbs and fry for a further few minutes. Add ale, plus a little water and gravy granules until a thick gravy forms. Simmer for 30 minutes. In the meantime, boil potatoes, drain and mash, adding chopped spring onion. Place hot steak mixture in a pie dish, ladle mashed potato over top, decorate with sliced tomatoes and serve with seasonal vegetables.

No fridge – use tinned stewing steak and even a packet of dried mashed potato if in the middle of nowhere.

Steamy Tabloid Trout

Fancy a romantic supper stuck out in the middle of nowhere with just a campfire, a loved one and stars for company…

1 tabloid newspaper	**1 pack couscous**
1 trout (prepared)	**Cherry tomatoes**
Sprig rosemary	**Green salad**
Lemon	**Butter**

Soak the newspaper in a bucket of water for 5 minutes. Open out and place trout in centre. Add a little rosemary, a knob of butter and a squirt of lemon juice inside the trout. Wrap newspaper around the fish to form a parcel and place on a grill over a BBQ or a camp fire for around 30 minutes. Turn the parcel every 15 minutes and keep wet by adding a little water, so that the fish steams inside. In the meantime, make the couscous, prepare the salad, open the wine and enjoy the evening.

Quick Spaghetti Bolognaise

A family favourite at home – and it only needs a 2 ring stove on camp…

1¼ lb. minced beef	Pinch mixed herbs
Spaghetti (sufficient for 4 people)	2 teaspoons rolled oats
1 large red onion (chopped)	4 garlic cloves (fresh or tube)
A few mushrooms (sliced)	Tomato puree (tube)
Beef stock cube	Olive oil
1 tin chopped tomatoes	Mixed salad and bread

Fry off the onion in the olive oil for a few minutes, then add the minced beef and stock cube to brown. Drain off any excess fat, then add the mushrooms, herbs, garlic and tomato puree to taste and fry for a further few minutes. Add oats and chopped tomatoes and simmer for 30 minutes, adding water as required. Boil the spaghetti in accordance with pack instructions, drain and arrange on individual plates. Add bolognaise mixture and serve with a colourful mixed salad and some Italian bread drizzled with olive oil.

No fridge – use tinned minced beef, tinned mushrooms and add a little paprika with the herbs.

Spicy Sausages and Rice

A delicious spicy one-pan version of sausages and mash…

Sausages from local butcher (2 each)	**1 tin chopped tomatoes**
Rice (around 2 oz. per person)	**Vegetable stock cube**
1 large red onion, chopped	**1 teaspoon curry powder**
1 stick celery (chopped)	**Water**

Brown the sausages in a large pan, then add the onion, rice and celery and cook for a few minutes, stirring all the time. Add the tomatoes, stock cube, curry powder and a little water, cover and cook on a low heat for around 20 minutes, until the rice is tender. Serve with bread and lashings of baked beans.

Chilli Mac

My children's favourite chilli - I discovered this recipe whilst serving with the American Air Force. A filling and easy way to combine chilli and pasta…

**1¼ lb. minced beef   1 large red onion (finely chopped)
1 tin chopped tomatoes   Handful mushrooms (chopped)
Beef stock cube   2 teaspoons rolled oats   Pinch mixed herbs
1 fresh chilli pepper (deseeded and chopped - or dried)
Chilli sauce   Olive oil   Dried pasta (sufficient for 4 people)
To serve – salad, cherry tomatoes and olive bread**

Fry off the onion for a few minutes, then add the mince, stock cube, herbs and chilli pepper to brown. Drain off any excess fat. Add tinned tomatoes, mushrooms, and rolled oats and simmer for 15 minutes. Check for 'heat' and add a little of your favourite chilli sauce to adjust. Simmer for a further 15 minutes. In the meantime, boil pasta with water according to pack instructions, drain and mix with chilli mixture. Serve with salad, cherry tomatoes and some olive bread.

No fridge – use tinned chilli and tinned mushrooms and fold into cooked pasta.

Camp Chicken Risotto

This is a delicious dish, using just one ring on your camping stove, so plenty of room to put that kettle on – or have you opened the wine already…?

4 breasts of chicken (cubed)   1 large red onion (chopped)
Handful mushrooms (chopped)   1 red pepper (sliced)
2 packs risotto rice (4 portions) + required water
1 vegetable stock cube   Olive oil

Fry onions in olive oil for a few minutes, then add chicken to seal. Add mushrooms and pepper and fry for a further few minutes. Add water, rice and vegetable stock cube and simmer until the water has been absorbed and rice cooked. Serve with some chunky bread.

No fridge – use sliced salami instead of chicken, which makes this an ideal dish to prepare if you are camping.

Stuffed "Roast" Peppers

This makes a delicious lunchtime snack or late evening supper…

4 peppers   4 oz. pack couscous (tomato flavour)
1 small red onion (chopped)
1 small jar sun dried tomatoes (drained and chopped)
A handful button mushrooms (chopped)
2 cloves garlic (crushed)   A little pesto sauce

Make up couscous in accordance with pack instructions. Fry onion and the garlic for a few minutes in a little oil. Add the tomatoes and mushrooms and fry for a further few minutes. Add pesto sauce and warm through, then combine with the couscous. Chop lids off peppers, scoop out seeds and white pith and fill with couscous mixture. Replace lids and wrap in foil. Place in BBQ or camp fire embers for 20 minutes and serve with chicken kebabs cooked on the BBQ grill and a green salad.

Local Fruit & Veg Kebabs

Visit the local Farmer's Market to find a few tasty treats to grill over the BBQ or camp fire for a satisfying locally grown lunch...

2 kebab sticks per person	**1 orange**
Selection of locally grown produce	**A squeeze of tomato puree**
1 jar local honey	**A little soy sauce**

Make up marinade by mixing freshly squeezed orange juice, with a tablespoon of honey, a little soy sauce and a squeeze of tomato puree. Place cubed fruit and vegetables in marinade and turn occasionally for a few minutes. Skewer onto kebab sticks, place over BBQ and grill until cooked, basting with any leftover marinade. Serve with some freshly baked local bread.

Many fruits and vegetables can be used but three good combinations are cherry tomatoes, strawberries and red peppers, or apple, courgette and celery, or cauliflower, pear and yellow peppers.

Mexican Camp Fire

*Cook this delicious Mexican chilli, sit around the camp fire and you
will be transported 1,000s of miles across the Atlantic…*

1 pack of wraps	**Chilli pepper, fresh or dried**
1¼ lb. minced beef	**Beef stock cube**
1 large red onion	**Pinch mixed herbs**
Handful mushrooms (sliced)	**Chilli sauce**
Tinned chopped tomatoes	**Lettuce (shredded)**
2 good pinches rolled oats	**Greek yogurt**
	Tin of refried beans

Fry off the onion for a few minutes, then add the mince, stock cube, herbs and chilli pepper to brown. Drain off any excess fat. Add tinned tomatoes, mushrooms, and rolled oats and simmer for 15 minutes. Check for 'heat' and add a little of your favourite chilli sauce to adjust. Simmer for a further 15 minutes. Heat the refried beans in a separate pan.

Load each wrap with lettuce, chilli mixture and a little Greek yogurt and serve with a selection of salads and refried beans.

No fridge – use tinned chilli (with some oats to thicken) and mushrooms.

Twenty-Four

Naughty Nacho Supper

It's late at night, glass of red wine in one hand,
a plate of naughty nachos to share in the other...

Big bag of tortillas (plain or cheese flavour best)
Large jar of salsa sauce
Red or green chillies (deseeded and chopped)
Gherkin (sliced)   Grated strong mature cheddar
Natural yogurt or sour cream

Sprinkle some cheese, gherkin and chillies over tortillas, drizzle with the salsa and yoghurt and serve with a glass (or two) of red wine for a long, relaxing evening watching the world go by...

Succulent Seafood Paella

*Camping by the coast? Then visit the local harbour for a selection of
freshly caught seafood to add to this delicious and quick paella…*

**1 lb. seafood of your choice   8 oz. short grain rice
A dozen large cooked prawns   1 large red onion (chopped)
1 red pepper (sliced)   3 large tomatoes (diced)
Cup frozen or tinned peas   2 oz. butter   2 garlic cloves
Pinch dried chilli   1 teaspoon mixed herbs   Pinch saffron
2 teaspoons paprika   Lemon (juice and grated zest)
4 fl.oz. white wine   Chicken stock cube and 1¾ pints water   Olive oil**

Cook the rice in the chicken stock and saffron until just tender – drain and
keep warm by wrapping pan in a tea towel.

Fry the onion in the olive oil for a few minutes, add the garlic, herbs, chilli and
pepper and fry for a few minutes. Add the seafood (but not the prawns), peas
and paprika and gently stir-fry for around 5 minutes. Add the lemon juice and
white wine and simmer for a further minute or two. Fold into the warm rice;
add the diced tomatoes, butter, lemon zest and a little seasoning. Scatter the
prawns over the paella and serve.

No fridge – use jars of seafood; drain and rinse before use.

Well Dressed Crab for Supper

Camping by the seaside, then grab a crab and enjoy this delicious supper…

2 dressed crab   **Butter**
Boil in bag rice for 4 people   **Mustard**
Handful cooked prawns   **Worcestershire sauce**
Paprika

In one pan, boil rice until cooked. In the meantime, melt a little butter, stir in the crab, a little mustard and a dash of Worcestershire sauce and heat gently, adding the prawns just before serving. Serve the crab on the rice and a dusting of paprika.

Nowhere near the sea – try using tinned crab.

Chicken Curry

A mild chicken curry is always a favourite with hungry scouts or family –
and adding a few accompaniments turns this recipe into a posh camping supper…

4 chicken breasts	Pilaf spice
2 onions	Madras or Balti curry paste
Handful mushrooms (chopped)	Nan bread
1 green pepper (sliced)	Poppodoms
1 tin chopped tomatoes	Selection of pickles
8 oz. rice	Bombay Mix

Fry off the onions for a few minutes, add the chicken and seal – drain off any liquid. Add the mushrooms and peppers for 2 further minutes, then the curry paste and fry for a further 5 minutes. Add the chopped tomatoes and simmer for 20 minutes and until the chicken is cooked through. In the meantime, cook the rice with some pilaf rice spice. Serve with a selection of accompaniments like Nan breads, popodoms, pickles, sliced tomatoes and Bombay Mix.

No fridge – use sliced salami or tinned chicken breast.

Vegetarian – substitute chicken for cubed courgettes, squash and aubergines and increase mushrooms.

Late Night Texas Hash

How about this heart warming supper dish for a chilly night sitting around the camp fire...

Large onion, chopped	**Tin chopped tomatoes**
Green pepper, sliced	**1 lb. cooked rice**
1 lb. minced beef	**Chilli powder**

Stock cube

Fry the onions for a few minutes, add the pepper and continue to cook until soft. Add the minced beef and brown, then stir in the tomatoes, cooked rice, a little chilli powder and the stock cube. Continue to cook for around 20 minutes until beef is cooked, adding a little water as required. Serve with chucks of crusty bread.

No fridge – use tinned minced beef.

Vegetarian – use tinned ratatouille.

Camp Corned Beef Hash

For a tasty supper dish, this surely has to keep the family quiet
for at least a few moments....

2 tins corned beef (finely diced)
4 large potatoes
1 large onion
A little mustard
To serve – brown sauce.

Cook the potatoes, drain and mash. Fry the onion until slightly burnt, then add the diced corned beef and a little mustard and stir-fry for a further 5 minutes. Add to the hot mashed potato, mix and serve with peas, thickly cut buttered bread and lashings of brown sauce.

Chinese Camp Stir Fry

*Fancy a Chinese takeaway but camping in a field miles from your nearest town –
try this recipe on your camping stove…*

4 chicken breasts (sliced)   1 red onion (sliced)
Handful of mushrooms (sliced)
Selection stir-fry veg (chopped and sliced where necessary)
(eg. peas, red peppers, baby sweetcorn, mange-tout, French beans, courgettes, tomatoes)
Small bag cashew nuts   1 jar favourite Chinese sauce
8 oz. rice

Fry off the onion in a little oil, add the chicken and seal. Put rice on to boil
and simmer for 20 minutes until cooked. Add the prepared vegetables and nuts
5 minutes before the rice is ready and stir-fry. Add the sauce, heat through for
a few minutes then serve with the rice.

No fridge – use tinned meat and a selection of tinned Chinese vegetables.

Vegetarian – replace chicken with selection of mushrooms.

Sweet & Sour Sausages & Rice

Who can resist this warming supper dish –
it reminds me of many wet and chilly evenings spent in a tent…

8 sausages from the Farmer's Market   1 large red onion
Fresh pineapple (around 10 small chunks)
Jar of sweet and sour sauce   8 oz. rice

Fry the onion for a few minutes, add sausages and fry until brown. Add the sweet and sour sauce and pineapple chunks to the sausages and gently simmer. In the meantime, boil rice, drain and serve on individual plates. Add sausages and pour over the remaining sauce.

No fridge – use good quality tinned sausages and tinned pineapple.

Vegetarian – use vegetarian sausages.

Farmer's Market Vegetarian Pasta

Pop down to the local farmers market and find some wonderful fresh vegetables and mushrooms to make this delicious and easy pasta dish…

Selection of fresh seasonal vegetables	**1 tin chopped tomatoes**
1 large red onion	**4 cloves garlic**
4 oz. mushrooms	**Pasta (sufficient for 4 people)**

Prepare vegetables in accordance with what you've bought. Fry onion and garlic in a little olive oil, add mushrooms, and vegetables and fry until almost tender, adding a little further olive oil as required. Add tinned tomatoes at last moment and heat through until hot. In the meantime, cook pasta, drain and place in large bowl. Add vegetable mixture and gently fold in – serve with a salad and chunky bread drizzled with olive oil.

In the middle of nowhere – use a tin of ratatouille and fold into cooked pasta.

"Bellybuttons"

Known as 'Bellybutton's' in my family, this fresh pasta with delicious pesto sauce dish is perfect for sitting outdoors one sunny summer's evening – and you can prepare it within 10 minutes, so not to miss all the al-fresco fun...

2 packs fresh pasta with ricotta cheese and spinach filling
1 large red onion (chopped)   Handful mushrooms (chopped)
1 small jar pesto sauce   1 small jar sun-dried tomatoes in olive oil
Salad and bread

Using some olive oil from the sun-dried tomatoes, fry the onions for a few minutes. Roughly chop the drained sun-dried tomatoes, add the mushrooms and fry – add the pesto sauce at the end and gently heat through. In the meantime, simmer the fresh pasta for 5 minutes (or as stated on the pack), drain and fold in the pesto sauce. Serve with a selection of olives, tomatoes and olive bread drizzled with olive oil.

No fridge – use dried pasta, tinned mushrooms and sliced peppers.

Omelette Rolls

*Out walking for the day? Then try this quick and easy way to make
some delicious egg-filled rolls for lunch on the go…*

4 eggs   4 rashers bacon (cut into small strips)
A little milk   1 tomato (thinly sliced)
Salt and pepper

Fry off bacon and tomato in a little oil. Break eggs into a bowl and whisk in
a little milk, seasoning to taste. Add to bacon and cook omelette until set.
Allow to cool and cut into segments. Fill rolls, adding a splash of tomato
ketchup.

Holiday Omelette

Pop down to the farmers market and buy some local free range eggs, some mushrooms, tomatoes, local cheese and a bundle of asparagus for this delicious and slightly spicy omelette

6 free range eggs   1 cup local cheese, grated
Handful mushrooms, sliced   2 large tomatoes (sliced)
4 spears of asparagus (if not in season, try leek), sliced.
Small red onion, sliced   Basil leaves
Chilli powder   Butter   Milk
Divide the ingredients and cook in two batches:

Fry the onions in a little butter for a few minutes, then add the asparagus or leeks, mushrooms, tomatoes, basil and a touch of chilli powder and continue frying for a few more moments. Beat the eggs with the grated cheese and add a little milk – pour over mixture, cover and cook until the eggs are set.

Serve with new potatoes and a green salad.

Blackberry Crumble

If you're lucky enough to be camping in the blackberry season, try this non-oven version of an old favourite – otherwise, pop down to the local farmer's market and see what fruit is available…

Large bowl of blackberries   **Mug breakfast muesli**
A few cooking apples   **Ginger biscuits, crumbled**
Yogurt

Wash and prepare fruit, then stew in a little water for 15 minutes. In the meantime, place the muesli mixture in the camp cooker grill pan and grill gently for 5 minutes, stirring at regular intervals. Placed stewed fruit in 4 individual bowls, sprinkle toasted muesli over top and serve with some natural yogurt and a sprinkling of ginger biscuits.

Camping in the middle of nowhere – use freshly picked fruit or a few tins of pie filling and crumble a muesli bar over the warm fruit.

Fruity Rice Pudding

Cooking rice for lunch? Then save some for this tempting supper dish…

Cooked rice (cold, enough for 4 small servings)
Small tub single cream
Assorted fruit

Mix the rice with cream, serve with cold sliced or warm stewed fruit of your choice.

No fridge – use tinned creamy rice pudding and omit the additional cream. Shame!

Ginger and Orange Pud

*Just because you're camping doesn't mean to say that
you can't enjoy a delicious creamy pudding…*

**1 large tub whipping cream   Packet of ginger biscuits
Tin mandarin segments   Flake chocolate bar or mini marshmallows**

Drain the oranges and whip the cream – then alternate with crumbled ginger biscuits and orange segments in a glass. Top with flaked chocolate or mini marshmallows.

Yummy Fruit Custard

Need a quick and easy pudding following a hard day's lazing around the camp site?
Then try this yummy delight…

1 can fruit pie filling (cherry works well)
2 cans custard   A few marshmallows
Chocolate flake bar

Just gently fold fruit into the custard, swirl and add a few chopped marshmallows. Serve with some flaked chocolate sprinkled over the top.

Freshly Baked Bread

The kids will love 'baking' this bread – and you'll enjoy eating it,
freshly baked and still warm from the camp fire or BBQ coals…

1 mug strong flour   A little water
A pinch salt   Jam
Some green twigs (about 3 feet long)

Place flour and a pinch of salt into bowl and add a little water until a sticky dough is formed.

Place a ping pong ball size piece of dough into floured hands and roll into a sausage shape. Wrap around end of green twig, twisting down for around 10 cm and seal end against twig with thumb. Place above embers of a camp fire of BBQ for around 5 minutes, turning slowly until golden brown all over. Allow to cool a little, ease bread off stick and fill hole with jam…. Delicious!

For gorgeous garlic bread, add a little grated cheese and garlic to dough before cooking, and omit the jam.

METRIC CONVERSIONS

The weights, measures and oven temperatures used in the preceding recipes can be easily converted to their metric equivalents. The conversions listed below are only approximate, having been rounded up or down as may be appropriate.

Weights

Avoirdupois	Metric
1 oz.	just under 30 grams
4 oz. (¼ lb.)	app. 115 grams
8 oz. (½ lb.)	app. 230 grams
1 lb.	454 grams

Liquid Measures

Imperial	Metric
1 tablespoon (liquid only)	20 millilitres
1 fl. oz.	app. 30 millilitres
1 gill (¼ pt.)	app. 145 millilitres
½ pt.	app. 285 millilitres
1 pt.	app. 570 millilitres
1 qt.	app. 1.140 litres

Oven Temperatures

	°Fahrenheit	Gas Mark	°Celsius
Slow	300	2	150
	325	3	170
Moderate	350	4	180
	375	5	190
	400	6	200
Hot	425	7	220
	450	8	230
	475	9	240

Flour as specified in these recipes refers to plain flour unless otherwise described.